Computer Networking Beginners Guide

The Complete Basic Guide to Master Network Security, Computer Architecture, Wireless Technology, and Communications Systems Including Cisco, CCNA and the OSI Model

© Copyright 2019 by **Kevin Morgan**

All rights reserved - © Copyright 2019 by Kevin Morgan

No part of this guide may be reproduce in any form without permission in writing from the publisher except in the case of brief quotations embodied in critical articles or reviews.

Legal & Disclaimer

The information contained in this book and its contents is not designed to replace or take the place of any form of professional advice; and is not meant to replace the need for professional advice or services, as may be required. The content and information in this book has been provided for educational and entertainment purposes only.

The content and information contained in this book has been compiled from sources deemed reliable, and it is accurate to the best of the Author's knowledge, information and belief. However, the Author cannot guarantee its accuracy and validity and cannot be held liable for any errors and/or omissions. Further, changes are periodically made to this book as and when needed. Where appropriate and/or necessary, you must consult a professional before using any of the suggested remedies, techniques, or information in this book.

Upon using the contents and information contained in this book, you agree to hold harmless the Author from and against any damages, costs, and expenses, including any legal fees potentially resulting from the application of any of the information provided by this book. This disclaimer applies to any loss, damages or injury caused by the use and application, whether directly or indirectly, of any advice or information presented, whether for breach of contract, tort, negligence, personal injury, criminal intent, or under any other cause of action.

You agree to accept all risks of using the information presented inside this book.

You agree that by continuing to read this book, where appropriate and/or necessary, you shall consult a professional before using any of the suggested remedies, techniques, or information in this book.

Table of Contents

INTRODUCTION 5
   What is wireless technology? 5
CHAPTER 1. • Wireless Communication Technologies 7
CHAPTER 2. • Mobile Communication Systems 15
CHAPTER 3. • Wireless technology challenges 27
CHAPTER 4. • Network Protocols 29
   1) TCP and UDP 29
CHAPTER 5. • Wireless Technology Security 39
   What is wireless network security? 39
   Types of wireless network security 40
      Wi-Fi Protected Access (WPA) 41
      Wired Equivalent Policy (WEP) 42
CHAPTER 6. • Features of Wireless Network Security 47
CHAPTER 7. • Security Issues in Wireless Networks 57
CHAPTER 8. • Wireless Network Computer Architecture ... 63
   Components of wireless communication 63
   Wireless Application Protocol (WAP) 67
CHAPTER 9. • Security architecture 71
   Site Planning and Project Management 76
CHAPTER 10. • Cellular Wireless Networks 87
   Features of cellular network systems 87
   Shape of cells 89

Frequency Reuse 90

The Evolution of Cellular Networks 91

    1G 92

    2G generation 93

    2.5G 96

    3G Wireless Systems 98

    Challenges of 3G Wireless Systems 99

    4G Generation 100

    5G Generation 100

Cellular System Architecture 101

CHAPTER 11. • Communication Systems and Network 103

Fundamentals of Transmission Systems: Technologies and Applications 103

CHAPTER 12. • Cisco, CCNA Systems 107

CISCO networking technologies 107

Entry (CCENT) 108

Cisco home networking 109

Cisco Packet Tracer 110

CHAPTER 13. • The OSI model 111

CHAPTER 14. • Wireless Network Applications 119

Types of wireless networks and their applications 119

CHAPTER 15. • Wired Network Components 123

CONCLUSION 133

INTRODUCTION

You might have heard about wireless access points, wireless networking, and wireless computing. These different terms are all related to wireless technology. Of course, they are not the only wireless devices; there are a plethora of wireless devices and technologies in the modern era. However, what is wireless technology and what are wireless devices? These and several other related questions will be answered in this chapter. Firstly, let me briefly give you an insight into what wireless technology is.

What is wireless technology?

Thus, wireless technology refers to technology that is not powered by wires and physical cables. By implication, wireless technology covers the use of radio frequencies and signals for data transmission rather than the conventional mode of data transmission via cables and the likes. For instance, phone channels, the Internet, and communication use physical wires that are physically connected for data transmission. Thus, rather than follow the physical connection, wireless technologies make the connection of each node of a network to be done with radio waves, thus eliminating the use of cables and other devices used for physical connection.

Another transmission technique that falls in this category is light based-transmission. This technology does not depend on the use of physical wires for connection and is thus regarded as a wireless technology.

CHAPTER 1. • Wireless Communication Technologies

A computer network refers to a physical and virtual connection of nodes that allows sharing of resources locally and remotely if possible. Connecting to a computer network can be wired or wireless. The transmission of signals via radio waves as a medium. Wireless technologies exist in various forms such as infrared technology used in home electronic remote controllers, Bluetooth connection, cordless keyboard, and cellular phones. A wireless network concerns a digital network that connects nodes locally or remotely through infrared, radio waves and microwave technologies to share resources.

Benefits of Wireless Communication

- Reachability: With wireless communication systems, individuals can stay connected and reachable irrespective of your geographical location as long as the area is covered by the wireless signal. Think of cellphones and hotspots.

- Mobility: Through the wireless communications system, individuals can access information beyond their current location without the need for a wired connection.
- Maintainability: The relative cost and time spent to maintain a wireless network system are less compared to wired setup in most cases.
- Simplicity: It is easy and fast to activate wireless communication system compared to a wired network even though the initial setup cost can be high.
- New services: Short message service and multimedia service are some of the smart services that can be deployed on wireless communication systems.
- Roaming services: Through wireless connections, you can offer services anywhere making wireless highly flexible.

Local area, wide area, and metropolitan networks are examples of computer network types. The following diagram shows a computer network:

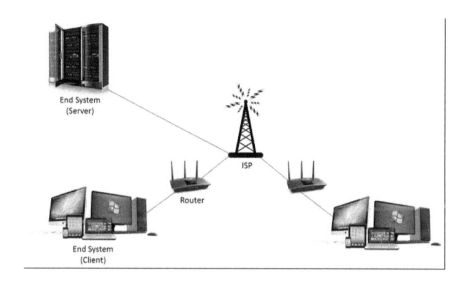

Wireless Network Topologies

The common ways to set up a wireless network are three, and these are:

    1. Point-to-point connection

A router is used to connect two networks such as two networks in two different buildings.

    2. Point-to-multipoint connection

In this topology, two or more local area connections are connected using a networking device such as a router.

    3. Ad hoc or mesh network

It is a network in which all nodes are directly connected and is independent of local area connection. Typically, a mesh network is connected using wired infrastructure.

Wireless technologies

Depending on their stage, wireless technologies can be classified. Every wireless technology is created to serve a particular usage. For each usage segment, the requirements are based on several variables such as bandwidth needs, power, and distance needs.

WWAN

It is known as the wireless wide area connection or network. This network is normally made to help you connect to the internet through a WWAN access card and a node. Compared to the rate of data transmission of mobile telecommunications, a wireless wide area connection provides a fast data speed. Examples of wireless wide area network include mobile and cellular networks that are built specifically on GSM and CDMA.

Wireless Personal Connection

A wireless personal area connection or network is similar to the wireless wide area network save that their range constrained.

Wireless LAN

The rendition of a wired LAN as a wireless network is known as WLAN. Even though it is referred to as WLAN, it also involves wired connections as everything cannot be wireless. For instance, the connection between the radio receiver and the main router is wired, and the connection between the main router and switches or other routers will be a wired connection.

The diagram below shows some common similarities in all the networks such as protocols, architecture, and topology/design.

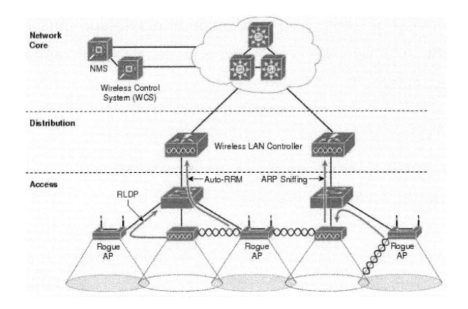

Wireless connections issues

Just like with any other type of technology, there are emerging and common issues when using wireless connections.

• Inadequate quality of service

Unlike the Internet, via wired services, wireless connections have issues when it comes to its quality of service, which is inadequate. Factors that worsen the quality of service include atmospheric interference and lost packets that tend to recur when using wireless protocol.

- Inadequate security

A paramount issue with the transfer of data over a wireless connection or network is that the basic measures to implement security with wireless communication such as SSID and WEP are inadequate.

- Limited range

However, the recent design of contemporary wireless connections allows for coverage of tens of miles, which makes this issue a less concern in modern networking of computers.

Wireless Broadband Access

Wireless broadband access technologies include 3G, WiMAX, and Wireless-fidelity among others that work cohesively to satisfy the needs of the customer. Equally important is that wireless broadband access is a point-to-multipoint system that constitutes a base station and subscriber equipment.

Equally important is that wireless communication systems are critical in areas that have challenges with terrain or where ensuring the security of physical cables is difficult. Wireless communication systems offer the most applicable way to keep such populations connected, and this makes wireless communication highly critical especially in the developing economies.

CHAPTER 2. • Mobile Communication Systems

Any form of communication you carry out with someone else with your mobile device is mobile communication. Aside from the examples above, mobile communication equally includes sharing files, videos, and other things via mobile devices.

In mobile communication technology, an area is divided into small cells. The division allows a frequency to be extensively used across a specific area. This is the principle that allows many people to communicate with their mobile devices simultaneously. This communication technique has tons of advantages, including reduced power usage, increased capacity, reduced interference, and larger coverage area.

Today, the popularity of wireless networks comes at a price: cybercriminals are always on the lookout for possible loopholes they can exploit to breach your security and compromise your data. Hence, it is a matter of urgency to find some ways to beef the security of your wireless network to prevent these criminals from breaching your security. Here are some security measures that can guarantee the security of your wireless network:

Understand the principle behind wireless networks

Understanding the principle behind how a wireless network works can be of help in safeguarding your wireless networks. If you want to go wireless, you need to connect a DSL modem, a cable, or any other access point to a wireless router. The router will then send a signal out through the air to the desired destination, which may sometimes be a couple of hundred feet away. Any device that is connected within the range will be able to pull the signal and have access to the Internet. With this understanding, you are likely more willing to take necessary precautions to ensure that no one has access to your network besides yourself and other authorized people.

Encrypt your wireless network

If you are using a wireless network at home or in your office, make it a point of duty to encrypt any type of information you want to transfer over the network to prevent eavesdroppers from gaining access to your confidential information. When you encrypt a data, it is scrambled into a code that others cannot gain access to. Encrypting your data is obviously the most potent way of shutting out intruders from your network.

There are two encryption techniques for the encryption: WPA and WEP. You should always use the same encryption for your router, computer, and other devices. If you need ideas, give WPA2 a try. This encryption technique is efficient and will secure your network against hackers. If you use wireless routers, they always have their encryption turned off. Turn this feature on to secure your network. You will find how to do this if you go through the router's manual. If you cannot find the instruction on the manual, visit the router company's official website for the instruction.

Limit access to your network

It is also your responsibility to ensure that only certain devices are allowed to access your wireless network. All the devices that are able to effectively communicate with a wireless network are automatically assigned a unique MAC (Media Access Control) address. Wireless routers are designed with a mechanism that they use for allowing devices that have specific MAC address to gain access to a network to ensure the security of your network. However, you should be cautious when using this security option. Some hackers and other cybercriminals have found a way to mimic MAC addresses and can easily infiltrate your network. Therefore, complement this security technique with some other effective network security techniques.

Secure your router

Your router is another device that deserves protection as well so that your wireless network will not be susceptible to cyber-attack via some loopholes in the security of your router. It is the responsibility of your router to direct traffic between the Internet and your local network. Therefore, protecting your router is the first step towards the protection of your entire network. If you leave your router unprotected, strangers may gain access to your network and thus access your personal and confidential information such as your financial information. If they have complete control of your router, you cannot predict what they will do with your network.

Change your router's default name

Your router obviously comes with a default name. This name is sometimes called SSID or the service set identifier. This is the name assigned to the router by the manufacturer. To increase the security of your wireless network, it is advisable that you change this default name and give the router a unique and difficult-to-guess name. Also, do not reveal this name to anyone. If you are the only person with access to the default name, it is almost impossible for the router to be subjected to a security breach.

Change the router's default password(s)

Just as the router comes with a default name, it also comes with a default password or a group of passwords. This password gives you the freedom to set up the router as well as operate it. Hackers are familiar with the default passwords and can use the knowledge to hack your router and gain access to your network if you leave the default password(s) unchanged. Make the password change for both the "administrator" and "user."

The rule of thumb stipulates that you use a combination of letters and numbers, known as alphanumeric characters, as well as long and difficult-to-guess passwords. It is advisable that you use a minimum of 12 characters for your password. You may also include lowercase and uppercase letters. The more complex your password, the more difficult it is for hackers to break. If you are unsure about how to change the password, visit the router company's website, and you will be guided through the process.

Do not always log in as administrator

After you have successfully set up your router, do not keep yourself logged in as administrator. Rather, you should log out immediately if you are not using the router. This will reduce the risk of being piggybacked on during your session in order to have access to your login details and take control of your router. That may have a dire consequence on your network.

Turn off "Remote Management" features

The reason for this security measure is obvious. Some routers' manufacturers offer the option to keep the remote management option turned on in order to provide you with technical support when necessary. Sadly, leaving this option turned on is synonymous to making your financial information available to the public. Hackers may capitalize on the feature to gain access to your router and, invariably, your network. On the other hand, when you leave this feature turned off, controlling your network from a remote location is impossible.

Always update your router

In order for your router to work effectively and be secure, the accompanying software must be regularly updated to fix bugs and other issues. Before setting up your router, visit the router's website to see if you can get the updated software that you can download. It is a course of wisdom to register the router with the manufacturer as well as sign up to receive regular updates to ensure that you are kept in the loop whenever there is a new software version.

Secure your computer

Regardless of the security measures you adopt for your router and other devices that are connected to your network, it is imperative that you secure your computer too. For instance, you can use some protections such as antispyware, antivirus, and firewall to fortify the security of your computer. Remember to keep the software up-to-date as well. Some valuable security tips include using a strong password for your computer and using up-to-date antivirus, antispyware, and firewalls. Do not forget to enable 2-factor authentication as well. Read this article: "**Computer Security**" for more practical tips that will help you keep your computer safe and secure from potential cybercriminals.

Log out of connected apps

If you access your network via an app, do not keep the app open when you are not using the app. Log out immediately and log in again whenever you want to access the network with the app. Why should you go through this process of logging in and out frequently? Remember that you can lose your phone or have it stolen at any time. Keeping the app open allows others to access your network via the stolen or lost phone. To further increase the security of the network through the app, adopt the password tips. Use a strong password that hackers will have a challenging time hacking so the chances of others gaining access to your network through your app are drastically reduced.

Password your phone

While password-protecting your app is a good idea, think about making your phone inaccessible to others as well. Protecting your phone will create the first barrier against unauthorized access to your phone and your network. I have given a list of practical tips for creating strong and difficult-to-hack passwords. Go through the chapter again and implement the tips. The stronger your password, the more difficult it is to hack your phone and access sensitive information that may be used against you or your network.

Reduce the range of your wireless signal

This is another effective security option you should consider. This is applicable to users whose wireless routers have a very high range while the users are using small spaces for operation. If you are in that group, decrease the signal range. There are two ways to do this. You can either change your wireless channel or change your router's mode to 802.11g rather than the conventional 802.11b or 802.11n. Alternatively, you can place the router in some secluded places such as inside a shoe box or under a bed. You can also wrap a foil around its antennas to perfectly restrict its signals' direction.

Stay under the radar

To hide the visibility of your network and stop your wireless network from broadcasting its presence, disable the router's Service Set Identifier (SSID) to make it "invisible." This will prevent strangers beside your business or home from being aware of the network and its name. This will also reduce the number of people who may be interested in gaining access to your network.

Turn off the network when not in use

Some experts consider this as "the ultimate in wireless security measures." The reason for this assertion is not far-fetched: if you shut your network down, most hackers will certainly be prevented from breaking in. While it may be impractical to keep switching the network off and on frequently, it is still practical to do it occasionally when you will not be using the network for a long time, perhaps when on vacation or when you will be offline for an extended period of time.

Have antimalware installed on connected devices

It is not out of place to take an inventory of the wide variety of devices connected to the network. When you have a full list of the devices, ensure that they all have antimalware installed on each of the devices for maximum protection against external invasion, especially in devices that can support the protection. Listed above are some effective ways you can close the door to your wireless network to the bad guys and thus prevent your network from being compromised. The suggestions here are practical and very easy to implement.

The tips discussed above have been tested and proven reliable over the years. Since precaution is usually better than cure, taking these steps to boost the security of your network is more rewarding and more effective than waiting until disaster strikes before running from pillar to post looking for a solution to the problem, so increase the immunity of your network and give cybercriminals a second thought about making attempts to breach your security. If you do not implement these tips, you are a sitting duck, an easy target for hackers.

CHAPTER 3. • Wireless technology challenges

Implementing wireless technology can be challenging. In a study conducted by senior IT executives, they discovered top five challenges that users of wireless technologies should contend with:

1. **Physical connectivity:** The issue of physical connectivity is one of the most important challenges that wireless technology has to deal with. In the study, the construction of some healthcare facilities posed a big challenge for the implementation of wireless technology. The specific challenges identified by the researchers include the difficulty of accessing broadband network and limitations on wireless signals on lower floors, older facilities in basement areas, and certain areas within the facility.

2. **Technology connectivity challenges:** Bandwidth availability was also identified as one of the greatest challenges inhibiting the implementation of wireless

technology in the health sector. When clinicians do not have bandwidth on their wireless network, they will not readily have access to their patients' information. That may have a negative impact on their efficiency and timely response to emergencies. Connectivity issues occasionally arise when applications are added to the network, especially if those applications are active in proprietary environments only. While the study concentrated on the health sector, its findings are a perfect reflection of all the other sectors of the global economy. Therefore, it is not out of reason that these challenges exist in the other sectors as well. The invention of wireless technology has proved to be of huge benefit to the users across the globe. Due to its wide areas of application, it has continued to proffer solutions to some of the networking issues associated with wired technologies and is responsible for the increased acceptance of the technology around the globe.

CHAPTER 4. • Network Protocols

1) TCP and UDP

In networking there are two main protocols which decide how the network applications need (ex: web server, file transfer, DNS etc.) to work. These two are known as TCP and UDP.

The thing is that we have choices. It all depends on the applications needs:

- If we want the application to work as fast as possible without **delay** (ex: **Voice, Video** over IP) then **UDP** is the perfect match

- If we are interested in the application delivering all the content, exactly as it is on the server (eg: a **website**), which implies a small delay then **TCP** is the perfect match

These protocols are called **TCP** (**T**ransmission **C**ontrol **P**rotocol) and **UDP** (**U**ser **D**atagram **P**rotocol).

TCP is considered a trustworthy protocol that guarantees the **retransmission** of **packets** in the event of their loss. It establishes a client-server connection (called three Way Handshake) using synchronization messages (**SYN**) or acknowledgment (**ACK**) for the receiving packets.

The disadvantage of TCP is the exchange of messages (establishing a connection, terminating it, sending SYN packets, confirming them - ACK) that **adds delay**. Networking applications such as HTTP (Web), FTP (File Transfer), SSH (Remote Connection) use this protocol.

UDP is the **exact opposite of TCP** (it does not retransmit packets, it does not establishes a connection before sending data, it does not reorders the packets etc.). UDP simply sends the packets from a specific source to a specific destination without being interested of the connection's status. The **advantage** of using this protocol is the **low latency** that allows for the smooth transition of the application with the lowest delay possible.

Thus, UDP is **suitable** for **real-time applications** (eg. Voice, Video traffic) that simply need to reach the destination as quickly as possible.

Because we were talking about real-time applications such as Skype, Facebook Live, CS Online Multiplayer, here are a few requirements for VoIP (**V**oice **o**ver **IP**) or similar delay sensitive apps:

- Delay: < 150 ms

o   Open CMD, type ping 8.8.8.8 and see the delay of every packet

- Packet Loss: < 1%

o   1 second of voice = 50 pkt of 20 ms audio each => 1% of 50 = 0,5; (this means that **at every 2 seconds we can lose max 1 packet**)

- Jitter (variable delay): < 30ms

2) Ports

A port uniquely identifies a **network application** (Web server, DNS, etc.) on a device in a network. Each port has an identifier (a number, ranging from **1** to **65535**).

When a PC sends a request (for a web page) to a server, this request will contain (among others) the following information:

Source IP**: PC**

Destination IP**: Server**

Source Port: 29813 (randomly generated by the Browser)

Destination Port**: 80**

In other words: The PC's browser (the source on port 29813) asks, from the server (Destination), for a web page (port 80).

Example - TCP ports

Now let's take a few examples where we can analyze and talk about what has been discussed in the sections of this chapter.

As you can see in Figure 4.1, there is a communication flow between two devices (source: 10.0.1.43, destination: 139.61.74.125).

The **source port** (**generated randomly**) in this case is 55881 (and most likely **was generated by a browser** -

Google Chrome, Safari, Firefox, etc.) and the destination port is **443** (**HTTPS**, a secure web application).

3) Network Applications

Here are a few examples of well known applications that you will encounter within a network:

HTTP

- **Description:** used for Web traffic (transports HTML files from server to client)

- Port: **80**

- Transport Protocol: **TCP**

HTTPS

- **Description:** used for **securing** the Web traffic

- Port: **443**

- Transport Protocol: **TCP**

FTP

- **Description:** allows the transfer of files between a client and a server

- Port: **20/21**

- Transport Protocol: **TCP**

DNS

- **Description:** finds the IP address of a domain name (ex: **google.com -> 172.217.18.67**)

- Port: **53**

- **Protocol de Transport:** UDP (client), TCP (server)

Telnet

- **Description:** remote access connection with a network device (Router, Switch etc.) or server

- Port: **23**

- Transport Protocol: **TCP**

SSH

- **Description: secured** remote access connection with a network device (Router, Switch) or server
- Port: **22**
- Transport Protocol: **TCP**

DHCP

- **Description:** dynamically assigns IP addresses (and other info) to all end-device in the network
- **Port:** 67/68
- Transport Protocol: **UDP**

SMTP

- **Description:** mail transfer protocol, used between mail servers
- Port: **25**

- Transport Protocol: **TCP**

IMAP

- **Description:** protocol for transferring mail from the server to the client (the emails will be stored on the server)

- Port: **143**

- Transport Protocol: **TCP**

POP3

- **Description:** transfers emails from server to client (and stores them on the client's PC)

- Port: **110**

- Transport Protocol: **TCP**

CHAPTER 5. • Wireless Technology Security

In this chapter, I will discuss the concept of wireless technology security extensively in order to assist you to have a deeper understanding of the concept, the potential security threats, and the practical security tips that can serve as preventive measures against these threats.

What is wireless network security?

This is the first question that most people ask. Well, there are different definitions for wireless network security. According to Wikipedia, "wireless security is the prevention of unauthorized access or damage to computers using wireless networks."

This definition by Technopedia also captures the concept well: "Wireless network security is the process of designing, implementing, and ensuring security on a wireless computer network. It is a subset of network security that adds protection for a wireless computer network."

These two definitions have obviously given you a better understanding of wireless network security that is otherwise known as wireless security. Wireless security is designed to protect a wireless network form malicious access attempts by potential hackers as well as from unauthorized personnel. Going by the name, you will realize that wireless network security is also done with a wireless switch/router or other wireless devices that by default can encrypt and secure wireless communication.

Sometimes, the wireless security may be compromised. In that event, the hacker is prevented from viewing the content of the packet or traffic in transit. More so, there are wireless intrusion systems that are responsible for detecting potential intrusions and preventing such an intrusion by alerting the network administrator whenever it detects any security breach.

Types of wireless network security

The increased global concern about the security of wireless networks has triggered the need for different security measures to be developed with the goal of reinforcing the security of wireless networks. Wireless network security can be achieved through some standards and algorithms that are specifically designed for that purpose. Some of these security measures are:

Wi-Fi Protected Access (WPA)

The Wi-Fi Protected Access is a security certification and security program for securing wireless computer networks designed to address some of the weaknesses in the Wired Equivalent Privacy (WEP). When you use WPA encryption for securing your Wi-Fi networks, you need a passphrase, otherwise known as a password, or a network security key. The passphrases are usually made up of numbers and letters. To establish a connection to the Wi-Fi network, the computer and whatever other connected devices must use the passphrase.

If you personally own the Wi-Fi network, it is advisable that you choose your own password when setting up the Wi-Fi network. Your password must be lengthy and be made up of alphanumeric characters and special characters to increase the security level of the password to prevent someone without the right authorization access to your network. When choosing a passphrase, you should also ensure that your passphrase is unique and cannot be easily guessed or cracked.

Wired Equivalent Policy (WEP)

WEP has been around for years. It's one of the security methods that have been around for years, especially for supporting older devices. The WEP security technique is not difficult to implement. You will trigger a network security key whenever you enable the WEP. The security key will encrypt any information that the computer shares with any other computer on the network. WEP was made known to the public by the Institute of Electrical and Electronics Engineers (IEEE) in 1979. This is a not-for-profit organization that has the responsibility of developing the right standards that can be adopted in electronic transmissions. There are two types of WEP. They are:

- **Shared key authentication:** This is a channel through which a computer can access a WEP-based wireless network. If a computer has a wireless modem, SKA will allow it to have access to the WEP network to enable it to exchange both unencrypted and encrypted data. For this authentication type to function efficiently, a wireless access point must match a WEP encryption key that has been obtained prior to the time of use by the connecting computer.

The connection process starts when the computer contacts the access point with an authentication request. In response to the request, the access point will generate a challenge text, a sequence of characters, for the computer. The computer will use its WEP key for encrypting the challenge text and later transmit it to the access point. After receiving the message, the access point will decrypt it and subsequently compare the result of the decrypted message with the main challenge text. If there are no mistakes in the decrypted message, the access point will immediately send the authentication code needed by the connecting computer to the computer. Then, finally, the connecting computer will accept the sent authentication code and thus is integrated into the network throughout the session or throughout the period when the connecting computer is within the original access point's range. On the other hand, if there is a discrepancy between the original text and the decrypted message, the access point will prevent the computer from becoming a part of the network.

- **Open system authentication:** The Open System Authentication (OSA) refers to a technique that allows a computer to gain unrestricted access to a WEP-based wireless network. With this system authentication, any computer that has a wireless modem can gain access to any network where it can receive unencrypted files. For the Open System Authentication to work, the computer's Service Set Identifier (SSID) should be the same with that of the wireless access point. The SSID refers to some well-arranged characters that uniquely assign names to a Wireless Local Area Network. The whole process occurs in just three stages.

First, the computer will send a request to the access point for authentication. When the access point receives the request, it will randomly generate an authentication code that is intended for use at the right time: during the session. Finally, the computer will take the authentication code and thus integrate into the network throughout the duration of the session and as long as the computer is within the range of the access point. You need a Shared

Key Authentication (SKA), a better and stronger authentication technique, if you find it necessary to transfer encrypted data between a wireless-equipped computer and the access point of a WEP network.

CHAPTER 6. • Features of Wireless Network Security

Everyone wants a fast and secure wireless network to meet their daily needs. Sadly, the evolution of technology comes with the difficulty of getting the security and performance you need. Even when you get it, it can be difficult to maintain and afford. The wireless system in existence now has a new set of features that the previous systems did not have. Therefore, regardless of the purpose of the network, there are certain features you should expect from a reliable wireless network. These are:

It must have high capacity loading balance

Originally, wireless networks were designed for coverage — nothing more. However, the proliferation of tablets, smartphones, laptops, and what have you has made it mandatory for the wireless networks in modern time to make room for capacity. Since there is a growing demand for both wired and wireless technology, high capacity load balancing must be incorporated into the network. This simply means that when one of the access points is overloaded, the system should be able to shift users to another access point determined by the available capacity.

Consider scalability

The need for more wireless devices will increase, as more people are aware of wireless networking and want to take advantage of the technology. Due to the increase, your network must be able to start very small — if that is necessary — but is scalable enough to keep expanding as the demand for the network keeps increasing. The expansion should cover capacity and coverage without the need to overhaul the entire network or build a new one entirely. The reality is that if you do not see any feasible need for the expansion today, you will see it in the future.

Network Management System

In contrast to what wireless was a couple of years ago, today, it is more complex with some hundreds or thousands of switches, access points, managed power, firewalls, and a couple of other components. Managing such a network with probably thousands of components can be quite challenging. You must find a very smart way to manage the entire network as a centralized network. When you deploy a network management system, you will have the needed ability to manage your network efficiently.

The ability to measure performance is a must-have

Users of the network will always have increasing expectations. It is important that you do everything possible to measure your performance from the perspective of your end-users. Thus, you must be able to see all end-users in real time. This will give you an insight into the type of devices these users are using, the type of applications they are running on the network, and the different status of all the networking components with the potential for affecting how those devices are used. Additionally, you must know how to run proactive tests that will enable you to see potential problems in advance and take precautionary measures against them.

Web application/content filtering

There has never been a time when network security needs to be aware of applications as a preventive measure against threats than now. This makes it a necessity for you to have application filtering incorporated into your network. The application filtering will protect your users from hazardous content that may pose a big threat to the network. It is also necessary for preventing potential performance issues in the system.

Network access control

Network access control is known in some quarters as mobile device registration. It is crucial to the network that you must have a reliable and secure method that you can use for registering your device. The method must also prove valuable in preparing security for other users' devices. It is network access control's responsibility to control the assigned role of each user as well as enforce some policies. With the network access control, each user can register himself or herself to the network. This is a very useful addition to the network and will give the users a memorable user experience.

Role Based Access Control

With Role Based Access Control (RBAC) you are allowed to assign roles to users based on some factors such as where, how, what, and when a device or user tries to access your network. Once you have successfully defined the end-user or device, you can enforce access control rules or policies. Leaving your network open to all can have an adverse effect on your network.

Ability to communicate with some devices

A secure wireless network must be able to communicate without much fuss with both 5GHz and 2.4GHz devices. Some devices such as Bluetooth, baby scanners, microwaves, and a host of other modern devices are known for their interference with network users on the 2.4GHz devices. This makes it a "crowded spectrum." Since a wide range of devices are still operating in the 2.4 GHz spectrum, you must have dual radio access points for managing users on both the 5GHz and 2.4GHz simultaneously.

Indoor/Outdoor coverage options

Although you may initially feel that you only need the network for indoor use, you may discover that you need it for outdoor purposes later. For instance, your wireless system must have the ability to add outdoor coverage to courtyards, parking lots, and so on. For instance, you may sometimes have one or two things to do over your network, and you may consider using your patio. If you do not activate this option, you will be incapacitated, as you cannot do anything on the network outside your home.

Application polarization

Application polarization is another important feature that a secure network must possess. This is your network's ability to ensure that applications that you have assigned a mission-critical status to are guaranteed the performance levels assigned to the applications. In essence, your business can make sure that the most important applications for your business and operations are not denied whatever they need to perform at the expected level, regardless of whether less critical applications are equally using the network simultaneously.

If your network lacks this basic feature, you simply cannot control the balance between recreational and business applications. There are also no ways you can make sure that the mission-critical systems and processes have access and can maintain the right performance they really need.

Mobile device management

You can imagine the number of mobile devices that will have access to your wireless network. What about the thousands of other applications that will be running on these thousands of mobile devices? The question is: how are you going to manage all these mobile devices and applications, considering the rate at which different devices are used in your business?

The mobile device management feature will be handy as it can offer you a good control of what you can do to be able to manage access to the programs and applications. If your device is stolen or lost, the mobile device management feature allows you to wipe the device off remotely.

Roaming

Some of the challenges that people have to contend with as they move from one place to another are slower speed, dropped connections, or any other type of disruption that may affect the network negatively. With the roaming feature, you do not have to worry about these issues because the wireless network is mobile-first. Being mobile places a huge responsibility on you; your users will not be satisfied with all these connection issues but will want to have the same high-level performance irrespective of their locations or whether they are in motion. Simply put, when you are planning for a wireless network, you are invariably considering roaming. This feature allows the end-users to move from an access point to another one successfully without a connection break. For instance, a student should be able to access his or her social media page while moving from one class to another.

Switching

A network switch is also a feature that cannot be overlooked. It acts as your network's traffic cop, ensuring that every device and everyone gets to their destination. For a couple of reasons, this feature is beneficial to the network. The switches will help your network's traffic flow more efficiently. It will also reduce unnecessary traffic and ensure that your traffic is heading towards the right direction. Be aware that performance issues may also arise from chock points or bottlenecks caused by using outdated switches or the wrong type of switches. Whether you are using a network or updating the current one, you simply must not ignore your switching. It has a huge impact on the network.

Adaptive radio management

You will find it extremely difficult to find technical expertise, aside from being expensive. It may take you a couple of years of training and the experience garnered over time to have an idea of the best way to get it right; this involves money and time most businesses can't afford. Adaptive radio management helps you maximize your network's performance to help you offer your end-users the best service. This is tantamount to having a Wi-Fi or an RF expert on your site and performing the same services. This ARM performs its operation by accessing the access points to collect valuable RF data from the access points. It subsequently uses the data for making intelligent decisions about channels, power levels, air-time freshness, roaming, and even client-loads.

Redundancy

Downtime ranks high among moral and productivity killers. If your Wi-Fi breaks down, everything else goes down with it. Your network needs an amount or level of redundancy determined by your needs and your environment. For instance, a hospital environment naturally needs something better than what a coffee shop needs. Nevertheless, both will need an impressive backup plan for future use.

CHAPTER 7. • Security Issues in Wireless Networks

The application of LAN in different environments has gradually increased the risk of wireless networks attacks. There are a couple of reasons for the increased rate of attacks aside from the proliferation of LAN. Here are some of the basic security threats you might have to deal with when running wireless networks are:

1. Denial of service

If you are familiar with the concept of network security, you may have come across this concept. Denial of service is a very simple and effective network attack because it doesn't have many requirements but only requires restricting access to the network service. If a hacker wants to expose you to denial of service, he or she will send a large amount of traffic at your network. Note that a single machine cannot handle the huge amount of traffic needed to have an appreciable impact on the target device.

There are other effective ways that access to network services can be denied aside from traffic flooding. If you are using wireless networks, denial of service can be easily done by using a wide range of techniques to interfere with the signal. For a wireless LAN on the 2.4GHz band, some simple things such as when a point is competing on a channel or an open microwave can easily interfere with the signal. Since the 2.4 GHz band has a restriction — it cannot exceed 3 non-overlapping channels — a potential hacker only needs to interfere with the three channels, and that will ultimately lead to denial of service.

This service denial attack can also be used with a rogue access point. For instance, a hacker can set up a rogue access point in a channel that is not in use by any legitimate access point. If this is done, a denial of service attack can then be launched at the currently used channel. This will cause the endpoint devices to embark on a re-associating process with a different channel that is in use by the fake access point.

2. Passive capturing

Unlike in the rogue access point security threat where physical access is a requirement for the effectiveness of the network, in passive capturing, getting physically connected to the network is not a requirement. The potential hacker only needs to get within the range of his or her target wireless LAN. When the hacker is close enough to the network, the hacker can then listen to the network and capture data in the process. The captured data can be used for a wide range of things such as analyzing the network's non-secured traffic or make an attempt at breaking the existing security settings.

The vulnerable nature of a wireless network makes it almost impossible for users to prevent the passive capturing attack. As a preventive measure, you can only boost your network's security by implementing high-security standards. You can only achieve any success here if you use some complex parameters for the security. In a nutshell, a wireless network has the primary responsibility of providing users with easy access. The ease of access opens the door to a problem: the network is more open to attacks. The best security measure is to increase your vigilance. Always ensure that your network's security is up-to-date and adapted to the changes in technology. This will help you ward off potential hackers as your network enjoys improved security.

3. Rogue access points

Rogue access points are otherwise known as Ad-Hoc networks. It is one of the most potent techniques used by attackers for targeting wireless networks. The attackers will set up a fake access point in a location within the reach of the original wireless LAN. The objective of setting up such a rogue access point is to deceive some of the original devices into connecting with the rogue access point and ignore the legitimate one. To make this threat effective, the attacker must be able to have physical access to the network. This is important because the user must be able to perform his or her regular activities on the network to ensure the effectiveness and long lifespan of the attack.

If an attacker has unrestricted access to a physical port, he or she can connect the access point to the physical port. This allows other devices to connect with the fake access point and take advantage of that connection for data capturing for a long period of time. This underscores the importance of restricting access to your network. The lower the number of people that can have physical access to your network devices, the lower your risk of becoming vulnerable to attacks through rogue access points.

4. Configuration problems

Many wireless network vulnerabilities are as a result of configuration problems. The problem arises from the zero-security configuration that comes along with shipping by many consumers or SOHO grade access points. Without the security configuration in place, any user can set up any device without much time and gain access to the network through the devices. However, these users also make their network open to external users even without any further configuration. Some of the other configuration challenges include weak security deployments, weak passphrases, and using the default SSID. I have already warned you about the dangers of using the default SSID; to boost the security of your network, the SSID should be changed immediately.

CHAPTER 8. • Wireless Network Computer Architecture

If you have paid attention to this book up to this moment, you will probably have got an improved understanding of what a wireless network is. Over the last couple of years, the world's dependence on this technology has continued to increase. Today, kids as young as five years old and the aged are now using different portable devices with an Internet connection that enables them to perform a wide range of activities such as communicate with people, check their email, or browse the web. Now, you can begin to ask how these networked devices work. How do portable devices receive data? These and other related questions will be answered in this chapter.

Components of wireless communication

Wireless communication has a lot of protocols, and each of these protocols has its unique criteria and specifications. These protocols try to achieve some general goals and characteristics. I will talk extensively about these protocols later in the chapter. However, these protocols follow the following guidelines:

- **Unlimited range and roaming:** The user has unrestricted movement and thus can have access to the network regardless of his or her geographical location. Thus, the user can still receive or send data irrespective of his or her distance from the network's base provider.

- **Host reconfiguration:** When changing environments, a protocol should be able to reconfigure the network automatically according to the prevalent network in the vicinity. For instance, if Mr. A with his mobile device enters a place where Bluetooth network is set up, his device will automatically configure itself to make use of the set up. When Mr. A gets home to his own setting that is quite different from the Bluetooth network he used a couple of minutes ago, the device will immediately shift to the network at Mr. A's house.

- **Delivery guaranteed:** Users are guaranteed of getting their data and messages delivered, not minding where the users are located. Even if the user turns off his or her device, the message will be delivered whenever the device is turned on again.

- **Dynamic encapsulation:** A protocol should also make it possible for a mobile host to be registered with its base agent by using a logout and login request. The goal is to prevent logins from being forged.

- **Dependability of notification:** This is another important guideline. Users should not be kept in suspense but should rather be notified whenever data is sent to them to prevent unnecessary data negligence out of ignorance of data delivery.

- **Host mobility:** A host may contain all its settings such as Subnet Mask, IP address, and Gateway address on a network. What happens if the host decides to change its location? This automatically means that it must change all its settings to reflect its new location while it simultaneously informs others of its relocation. A host that enjoys flexible mobility can change its location as it pleases without the extra burden of informing others of its relocation. Thus, it still has the communication line with its host open, although it has relocated.

- **Numerous connectivity options:** Both the senders and the receivers are not restricted to a single connectivity. Rather, they have a wide range of options to choose from. This allows each user to choose the options that best suits his or her needs.

- **Priority alerts:** Since the users will be receiving tons of data and messages, it is very important that they know the data and message that should top the priority list. The right protocol should also have the ability to put high-priority data traffic under control swiftly.

- **Communication:** Communication ability is one of the most important guidelines that a protocol must incorporate to deem it fit for use by users from all walks of life. A protocol must enable users to communicate with each other via their portable devices. Each device will be powered by some user-friendly applications.

Now that we are through with the guidelines that ensure that the protocols provide the users with the best services, it is high time we discussed some of the communication protocols.

Wireless Application Protocol (WAP)

Over the years, the Wireless Application Protocol has gradually set the pace for communication between server applications and their clients. That's exactly the function of the Wireless Application Protocol. For instance, WAP allows communication between a server and a cellular phone. WAP is now the link between the mobile world and the Internet, bridging the gap between these two giants. WAP itself is designed with the same model as the Internet. The portable devices that are using WAP are designed with a browser software connected to a WAP Gateway. It is this software that is responsible for sending requests to the web server to receive data. This data can be an email or a web page. When the data is received, its content will be forwarded to the portable device where it is received and viewed. This depends on the portable device's capability to receive data as well as view it.

WAP was founded by the big players in the technology industry, Nokia, Ericsson, Phone.Com, and Motorola. These companies formed WAP in 1997 and later created the WAP forum with the goal of using the forum to ensure strict adherence to the WAP specifications. Some of the WAP specifications that they are bent on preserving include scripting, micro browsing, a layered protocol stack, and wireless telephone applications. As previously mentioned, WAP ensures the connection between the wireless world and the Internet. Therefore, there are two important things about the connection that must be addressed. These are:

- **HDML vs. HTML vs. WML:** These are three important technologies behind Internet communication. HYPERTEXT Markup Language (HTML) is a scripting language used exclusively for translating data to a web browser so that a user can have free access to the data and view it. There is also the Handheld Device Markup Language (HDML). As the name suggests, this scripting language deals with portable or handheld device applications. A typical example of such device applications is a micro browser. The third member of the group is Wireless Markup Language (WLM). This scripting language is a derivative of HTML and is used together with WAP for incorporating WAP features.

- **How to incorporate WAP:** Incorporating WAP can also be done automatically. For instance, if a user has a WAP-compliant phone, he may decide to look something up on his phone's mini browser and automatically requests for the data. This request will be forwarded to his mobile service network's WAP Gateway. The network's server will retrieve the requested information in HTML format. Sometimes, WML format may be used provided that the server has the ability to use the WAP Gateway's filter. A simple request will be sent via the Gateway, while the Gateway will send the requested data to the user for viewing on his or her browser.

CHAPTER 9. • Security architecture

Security refers to the state of being free from threats and danger. Information security is the state of being safeguarded against the unwarranted use of data, particularly electronic information, or the precautions in place to accomplish this. The growing use of the internet and mobile applications has posed a great risk to information security.

The set of ad hoc actions can be modified depending on the way information security is viewed. These actions can be modified by making use of adaptive solutions, applying behavior that suits business requirements and coordinated approach to principles.

This may result in the enhancement of strategic programs and reduced budgets. Therefore, there will be an increase in businesses that implement compliance with regulations using an inclusive program.

The advantages of information security architecture may be familiar with security professionals but creating and restructuring information security architecture is a challenging activity. Information security field has sophisticated dynamics, but it needs a significant investment of human labor to create a systematic architecture.

To make sure that such a commitment can be maintained for an extended period, clearly written down rules for security experts have to be followed strictly. Industries' models and reference standards are being modified every day, but the creation of universal business-wide information security remains unpredictable. Because of these modifications, it is recommended for businesses to come up with and maintain their Information Security Architectures, by employing the use of suitable industry articles and models.

Almost 40 percent of large businesses have invested heavily in information security benefits. However, most of these investments are concerned with technology. The growth is estimated to grow to 60 percent in the following years, and the designs will be more strategic and not just centered on technology.

The following are the merits of information security architecture:

- Businesses always get a shared vision for information security across their departments from Information Security Architecture. Information security is implemented differently based on business the departments which have certain motivations and objectives.

- Executives usually take information security as part of their legal and strategic management duties. Business managers are exected by Information Security Architecture to be responsible for the integrity of their applications and data.

- Information Technology companies are required to provide security services to companies while employees are required to demonstrate good corporate citizenship. A shared vision in companies is vital, given the impact, reach, and scale of information security in all sectors of business.

- Businesses may be helped by the Information Security Architecture to align their activities, strategies, and initiatives to accomplish the common vision. This is important in discouraging dormant activities in the business, promoting consistency, and increasing re-use of business resources. Consequently, there will be improved progress and speed towards the accomplishment of the shared vision.

- Information Security Architecture enhances understandable and common language for communication by coming up with simple definitions of information security. Many security terms which have been used for many years are usually commonly used outside the information security field. Besides, as the field of information security continues to change, new terminologies will come into existence.

Teamwork and cooperation are necessary to ensure that information security is useful in most businesses. Therefore, it is essential for all branches of the company to possess a shared and similar comprehension of the terms used in information security architecture.

Moreover, information security architecture helps business managers to be familiar with the nature of the language that businesses employ in communicating externally; that is, the words used by suppliers and some vendors to communicate.

Languages and definitions used in information security architecture can be challenging to understand because of the information security market. Consequently, information security architecture always gives a set of terms that can assist you to comprehend these terms.

Businesses that have applied information security architecture successfully have enjoyed many benefits. They have access to a platform that can assist them to comprehend the standard management tools, processes, and principles that are vital in implementing secure networks that are compatible with the business objectives and requirements. By doing this, businesses can select and have a perfect balance between consistency and flexibility.

Information security architecture assists business stakeholders in understanding information about regulatory compliance, risk management, and security. Majority of the regulators accept that addressing network security issues is an endless and continuous activity. The most natural and easy way to deal with such problems is to record all the activities and find out the reasons why they were recorded.

Site Planning and Project Management

Project planning and requirements

After defining the project and appointing the project team, the next phase is the detailed project planning. Project planning is normally done by following the project management life cycle. It informs every person involved in the project what you intend to accomplish and how you will achieve your goals. The project plan is documented, project requirements and deliverables are defined, and the project schedule is made. It entails coming up with a set of plans to guide your team via the closure and implementation phases of the project. The plans developed during this phase will be of great help in managing quality, risk, modifications, cost, and time. They may also help you supervise staff and control suppliers to see to it that you finish the project before the deadline.

The aim of the project planning phase is:

- Coming up with the business needs
- Establishing resource plans
- Obtaining management approval before proceeding to the next phase

The fundamental processes of project planning are:

Procurement planning

Subcontracting by concentrating on vendors external to your business

Budget planning

You specify the budget cost to be spent on the whole project.

Risk management

You will be tasked with planning for possible risks by taking into account mitigation strategies and contingency plans.

Communication planning

Make use of all project stakeholders and use them to come up with the best communication strategy.

Resource planning

You can do this by indicating who will do a certain task and the specific time for the work to be done. Also, you can indicate whether there is a need for any special skills to do the task.

Scope planning

You should specify the in-scope needs for the project to make it easier for the work to break down the structure to be created.

Quality planning

It entails assessing the criteria of the quality to be used in the project.

Network requirements

For a network to operate efficiently, three fundamentals requirements must be present: the network must provide services, connections, and communication.

- Connections-they includes the software and the hardware or physical components. The physical components connect the computer to the network. The network medium and the network interface are the two important terms of network connections. The networking hardware that connects one computer device to another is called the **network medium**.

The physical component that connects the computer to the network medium and functions as an interpreter between the network and the equipment is called the **network interface card (NIC).**

- Communication- it establishes the regulations about how computer devices exchange information and understand one another. Computers must speak a common language to communicate effectively because they run different software. In the absence of shared communication, computers cannot exchange information successfully.

- Services- they are the utilities or things that a computer shares with the network. For instance, a computer may share specific files or a printer. Unless computers connected on a network can share resources such as files and printers, they will remain isolated although they will be connected physically.

Planning access point-placement

Accurate placement of access points is necessary to unleash the full potential and performance of wireless connections. In many enterprises, access points for local area networks primarily distributed in interior compartments. These access points were traditionally preferred and selected based on WLAN bandwidth, aesthetics, the feasibility of deployment, coverage, and channel re-use. In some instances, client preferences and deployment restrictions determine the access point placement location. For example, the placement of access points on floor perimeters may be illegal.

Note that it is not necessary to place access points precisely on the perimeter. Access points can be placed inside an apartment to offer better coverage of RF in addition to minimizing wastage of RF outside the apartment.

Using antennae to tailor coverage

It is necessary to offer coverage for a unique region that does not follow the rules and conventions you expect it to follow. Majority of the access points use omnidirectional antennas that radiate in all directions equally. Modifying the radio coverage pattern for certain, applications may be vital. This work is usually done by adjusting overage from an access point to match with a specific region or by boosting a signal to fill a hole. With the reducing cost of access points, customized tailoring coverage of antennas is not crucial as it was in the past.

Types of Antennas

All wireless NIC cards have antennas built-in internally, but they cannot be used if you plan to cover an office or any vast region such as a college or a campus. External antennas are used as access points if you plan to cover a wide area. You should pay attention to the following features when considering specialized antennas:

- Gain
- Antenna type
- Half-power beam width
- Vertical antennas

802.11 Network Analysis

Sometimes, wireless connections break. Wireless local area connection enhance productivity, but they pose a great danger of total outage because the bandwidth is often overloaded. After creating a wireless local area connection, network managers should investigate any possible problems that may be experienced by the user.

As with many types of networks, a trusty network analyzer should be used by the network engineer to identify any possibilities of the network outage. Network analyzers exist for wired networks and can still be used to troubleshoot wireless connections. For success in analyzing the wireless connections, you require to view the airwaves and also try to use a network analyzer tool that is designed specifically for the same reason.

802.11 Tuning of Performance

Initially, wireless network managers somehow enjoyed a free ride. Wireless is cool and new, and most clients don't know what kind of service they should wait for. Moreover, most wireless connections are dependent logically to existing wired networks. 802.11 standards were designed to add functionality to existing local area connections but not to substitute them. When the wired local area connection is the main network, clients can get the work done without the wireless network, and it is viewed as less important. Most likely, your major problems are placing your access points so you can have network coverage everywhere you desire, keeping your security configuration updated, and installing required drivers.

Even though wireless connections have a specific way of growing, and customers have a way of demanding for better services as time goes by. The performance of your network "out of the box" is always fairly poor, even if no one but you realizes. Changing the external environment (by doing experiments with external antennas and placement of access points, et cetera.) may do away with some problems, but others may be addressed better by making use of administrative factors. This section discusses in detail some of the organizational factors.

The Architecture of a Logical Wireless Network

Managing a wireless local area connection installation is an essential activity that cuts across numerous distinct professions. This section starts the discussion of wireless local area connections installation and deployment by considering the architecture of the network. Designing of a network is concerned about a balance or trade-offs among certain factors, such as performance, availability, manageability, and cost. Wireless connections are also concerned about the mobility of the network.

Such networks regularly support an existing wired connection. The wired connection may be sophisticated to start with, mainly if it covers many residences in a school setting. Wireless connections solely depend on the availability of a stable, fantastic, solid wired connection in place. If the current network in use is unstable, the probability is high that the wireless extension will fail because it may also be unstable.

This section discusses four methods for creating a wireless local area connection. All are considered based on the nature of the technical characteristics of the wireless local area connection that determines how you come up with a wireless network. In what ways do the characteristics of wireless local area connections affect the topology of the network? In addition to the 802.11 standards, what other factors and hardware are required to install a network successfully? How can the logical wireless network be built to ensure there is maximum mobility?

CHAPTER 10. • Cellular Wireless Networks

Cellular network is the technology behind personal communication systems, mobile phones, and wireless networking. This technology is developed for use in mobile radio telephones as a replacement for the high-power transmitter/receiver systems that were previously used in mobile telephony.

As a perfect replacement, cellular networks are designed with the right features that make it an efficient replacement that has taken wireless networking to the next level — especially in mobile communication. The awesome features include shorter range, lower power, and a higher number of transmitters that make data transmission faster and better. Let me give you a comprehensive list of the features of this amazing technology.

Features of cellular network systems

Wireless Cellular Systems has succeeded in solving the spectral congestion problem associated with wireless communication as well as increase the user capacity of wireless technology. These laudable achievements can be traced to the impressive features of the cellular systems such as:

- In a limited spectrum, it offers a very high capacity.
- Radio channels can be reused in different cells.
- A large number of users can be served by a relatively smaller number of channels within a coverage region.
- Communication is usually between the base station and mobile, not directly between the mobiles alone.
- Each of the base stations has a group of radio channels allocated to it in a small geographic area.
- Different channel groups are assigned neighboring cells.
- It also reduces interference levels to tolerable limits.

- Frequency planning or reuse.

Shape of cells

As previously mentioned, the areas covered by a cellular network are known as cells. Each cell is equipped with its own antenna for signals transmission in addition to having its own transmission frequencies. For data communication to take place in cellular networks, the receiver, base station transmitter, and control unit are all taken into consideration. The shape of each cell can be either hexagon or square.

Hexagon

This cell shape is considered the better of the two cell shapes. It is the more recommended of the two for data transmission because it offers easy coverage and can easily be calculated. These are the advantages of this cell shape:

- Equidistant antennas are provided.
- The distance from the center of the cell to the vertex is equal to the length of its side.

Square

In a square cell, there are four neighbor cells each at distance, d, from the cell while some other four are at another distance square root of 2 d from the cell as well. The square shape cells are the ideal shape under these conditions:

- If all the adjacent antennas are equidistant from each other.

- If you want to choose and switch to a new antenna. The square cell makes the switching pretty easy.

Frequency Reuse

Frequency reusing simply refers to a concept that involves the use of the same radio frequencies in a specific area. The areas have some considerable distance separating them and have reduced interference to the establishment of communication. Here are some of the benefits of adopting the frequency reuse concept:

- There can be communication within a given cell on any frequency.

- Escaping power is limited to adjacent cells only.
- Frequencies can be reused in neighboring cells.
- A single frequency can be used for multiple conversations.
- It allows between 10 and 50 frequencies in a single cell.

For instance, if **N** cells use **K** number of frequencies in a system, cell frequency can be calculated as **K/N** for each cell.

The Evolution of Cellular Networks

Telecommunication has continued to move at a very fast pace globally. The telecommunications industry is not relenting in its efforts to keep churning out one innovation after another. The innovation is also seen in the cellular network sector that has witnessed a huge transformation in recent years. The mobile industry has witnessed some generations that contributed in one way or the other to the popularity and acceptance of wireless communications. Here is a brief summary of these generations:

1G

Note that the names assigned to these signals are in reference to the age of the technology powering the signal. For instance, 1G refers to the first generation of the wireless signal. The 1G generation came into existence in the late 1970s and was made available to the general public in 1980s, although it is no longer in use. The 1G signal was just strong enough to make phone calls possible, but it wasn't strong enough for data transfer. The technology was slow compared with the current technology and had a shorter range as well. This should not be surprising because it was only used by analog networks. Some of the representative standards behind this generation include:

- **AMPS:** The Advanced Mobile Phone System was developed in the 1970s by AT & T Bell Labs. It was later deployed a couple of years later in 1983. The first of this system used omni-directional base station antennas and large cells. This was responsible for the limited number of users supported by this generation. The AMPS got wide acceptance and usage in some countries such as South America, Australia, US, and China.

- **ETACS:** The European Total Access Communication Systems shared some similarities with the AMPS, which made them almost identical to each other. The only difference is that the channel bandwidth in the ETACS has a scaling of 25kHz rather than the 30 kHz used by the AMPS.

2G generation

The 2G generation came about a decade after its predecessor. It was the mobile technology behind the Global System Mobile (GSM). It was a bit faster than the 1G generation as it offered up to 9.6kbps data rate per channel and was officially the first generation that offered a digital cellular network. Although the twoG offered sufficient network capacity to enable users to send data, it was not as powerful as to allow them unlimited data transfer. The only data that could be transferred conveniently was mostly text messages. Making online connections was still a big issue. It was still done via dial-up.

2G was based on the principle of digital modulation and digital voice coding. As an improvement over the 1G, it can provide some advanced call capabilities that can only be dreamt of by the 1G. For instance, it boasts of a minimum of 3-times increase in its overall performance and system capacity when compared with the 1G. Since the 2G was designed before the Internet became a household name, it supported limited date-service and voice-centric services such as fax and short messages. Its data rate was about 10kbps. The 2G wireless system also had some representative standards behind its operation. Some of these standards include:

- **GSM:** The Global Systems for Mobile Communications ranks high among its representative standards. Using a TDMA system, the 2G serves the European community as the pan-European cellular service and provides an array of network services such as fax, phone service, short message, and what have you. The generation has a better data rate of 24.7kbps.

- **USDC IS-136 (United States Digital Cellular):** This is a TDMA system without any compatibility issues with AMPS. Thus, it was not as limited as its predecessors because it supports 6 times more users than the 2G. Its performance was also a notch above it. The USDC shares the same frequency reuse plane, frequency, and base stations as its contemporary, the AMPS. In addition, it also can also be used for short messages in addition to providing access to VPN. To its credit, it has a better data rate of 48.6kbps.

- **IS-95 (United States Digital Cellular Standard):** This CDMA standard was also designed to work effortlessly with AMPS without compatibility issues as well. It works with AMPS though CDMA/AMPS base stations and dual-mode phones. With a capacity that is approximately 10 times the AMPS' capacity and a data rate of 14.4kbps, this is simply a good representative standard.

2.5G

The 2.5G was the first cellular service that allowed the services to always be "on." This technology did not require dial-up for operation but ensured that the users were always kept connected to enable them use the data or place a call at their convenience. Cell phone service providers capitalized on this and started billing their subscribers for the first time by the kilobyte rather than use per minute billing. The 2.5 G generation was extensively used in the General Packet Radio Service (GPRS) and the GSM Extension with Enhanced Data GSM Evolution (EDGE). GPRS goes on record as the first virtual data network that made extensive use of the Wireless Application Protocol (WAP). WAP could deliver up to 144kbps on its own and 384kbps when combined with EDGE.

Kudos to the brains behind the technology; they found a convenient way to use the 2.5G to perform at double the speed of the regular 2.5G. Nevertheless, the EDGE technology was still far below the proposed 3G.

Compared with the 2G, this generation makes a continuous connection to the Internet more than just a dream but a reality. It also gives its users access to high-speed data communications and can thus provide its users better overall performance. Some of the outstanding representatives of this wireless generation include:

- **CDPD (Cellular Digital Packet Data):** The CDPD provided the 1st and 2nd generation cellular systems with a reliable data service without an additional load of bandwidth requirement. Its packet channels are automatically available for idle voice channels. To its credit, it shares the same data rate as the 1S-136: 48.6kbps.

- **GPRS (General Packet Radio Service):** The GPS was based on the GSM. It allows many GSM radio channel slots to be dedicated to a single user. With a data rate between 56kbps and 114kbps, users are guaranteed uninterrupted Internet connection for their computers and mobile phones. Easy access to the Virtual Private Network (VPS) is another benefit of this standard.

- **EDGE (Enhanced Data Rates for GSM Evolution):** This standard was built on the improved modulation 8-PSK, which allows it to provide an awesome data rate of 384kbps, unlike the GMSK used in GSM that provides a lower data rate. EDGE is also known as EGPRS.

- **CDMA one (IS-95B):** This standard uses a CDMA radio channel to provide high speed data access to its users. It achieves this high speed by dedicating some of the multiple orthogonal user channels to specific purposes and/or specific users. It supports 115. 2kbps.

3G Wireless Systems

This generation was characterized by the High Speed Packet Access (HSPA). The HSPA was a one of the best IP-based Internet access and offered higher data rates than its predecessors. This generation made rates of 3Mbps and higher possible. The 3.5G technology even rose to the theoretical 14Mbps as a proof of the improvement this generation offered mobile users.

The 3G generation also allowed faster downloads and uploads, a necessity considering the need for video and pictures sharing. Yet, this technology has its challenges too. With a mobile device, a user can have access to simultaneous voice and data access with many people and can also enjoy multiple-megabit Internet services. You can also enjoy wireless access to the Internet wherever you are in the world through its seamless global roaming. This wireless system obviously includes the more advanced satellite networks.

Challenges of 3G Wireless Systems

- The 3G system is known for its high transmission rate. This implies a wider signal bandwidth than the channel's coherence bandwidth and thus, different fading characteristics will be experienced by the wide range of frequency components in the provided signal.

- The higher transmission rate and enlarged capacity imply that more efficient means of deploying available bandwidth will be required. The general implication on the system is that it needs to be reused more often than before.

4G Generation

This generation allowed the deployment of end-to-end IP network. It has gained significant popularity since its creation and is now widely used across the world. This generation is super fast and can deliver up to 100Mbps broadband speed, making it the fastest generation so far. It is as 250 times faster than its predecessor, the 3G cellular network.

5G Generation

The 5th generation wireless system is an improved wireless technology over the existing network technologies. The 5G generation has some impressive technologies, such as some millimeter wavebands in the ranges 26, 28, 38, and 60GHz. These wave bands can offer as much as 20Gbits/s (gigabits per second).

Another impressive feature of this wireless generation is the massive Multiple Input Multiple Output (MIMO) incorporated into the technology. MIMO offers an impressive performance that is reputable to be "up to ten times the current 4G networks."

Cellular System Architecture

The cellular system is driven by a simple architecture. Let me take you through the architecture of this powerful technology.

- **Radio Access:** This is the radio frequency-related signal processing and radio resource management. In essence, communication takes place from the mobile to the base station and from the RNC or BSC to the MSC.

- **Core Network:** The main part of the core network is the MSC or the mobile switching center. It is responsible for admission control, performing user authentication, billing, traffic control, network support, roaming, and maintenance.

- **Backbone networks:** The backbone networks are responsible for providing Public Switched Telephone Network (PSTN), a voice service, and emergency services. In order to benefit from the geographic coverage and service capabilities of wireless networks, the backbone networks and wireless networks must be connected together.

CHAPTER 11. • Communication Systems and Network

Behind successful wireless communication systems are these two powerful technologies: communication systems and communication networks. Let's take a good look at these two important technologies and see their contributions to the wireless communication world.

Fundamentals of Transmission Systems: Technologies and Applications

A typical example of transmission in communication is the sending of a signal from the sender to the receiver. For instance, a packet or block of data, an email, or a phone call can be sent from the sender to the receiver. Such signals are usually with limited duration. The transmission schemes and technologies refer to some physical layer protocol duties like:

- **Error control:** In telecommunication, error control is a technique that enables digital data to be reliably delivered over communication channels that are less than reliable. Most of the communication channels are prone to errors such as channel noise, and this may lead to the introduction of errors during transmission to the receiver through the source. Such errors are detected with the assistance of error detection techniques before they are corrected by another important technique, error correction, which allows the original data to be reconstructed in most cases.

- **Modulation:** In telecommunications, modulation refers to the process involved in conveying message signals in another signal with the potential for physical transmission. For instance, an analog audio signal or a digital bit stream can be conveyed in this form. The modulation is usually performed with a modulator. The goal of using analog modulation is the transfer of a low pass signal or analog baseband at a different frequency over an analog band pass channel. For instance, a TV signal or an audio signal can be transferred over a cable TV network channel or a limited radio frequency band. One of the most popular uses of the analog modulation techniques is the Amplitude Modulation (AM). In this technique, the amplitude of the carrier signal must be varied in correspondence with the modulating signal's instantaneous amplitude.

- **Equalization:** In the telecommunication world, equalization refers to the "reversal of distortion incurred by a signal transmitted through a channel." These equalizers are notably used for rendering the frequency response flat from one end to another end. An equalized channel has the input signal's frequency domain attributes of reproduced flawlessly at the output. DSL lines, telephones, and television cables take advantage of equalization to prepare their data signals in advance for transmission.

Equalizers have proved to be indispensable tools for the successful operation of analog broadcast television and other electronic systems. When used, there must be a preservation of the real waveform of any transmitted signal in addition to preserving its frequency content. Any phase delay or group delay between the components of a frequency are easily canceled out by equalizing filters.

CHAPTER 12. • Cisco, CCNA Systems

CISCO is unarguably the largest networking company in the world. The San Jose, California-based multinational technology conglomerate located in Silicon Valley has proved to be the leader in wireless technology with over three decades of experience in the field. CISCO is reputable for developing, manufacturing, and selling telecommunications equipment, networking hardware, and some other high-technology products and services. Since its acquisition of some subsidiaries such as WebEx, Jasper, OpenDNS, and Jabber, the company has also proved to be an expert in some specific technology markets such as domain security, Internet of Things (IoT), and energy management. Founded in December 1984 by two computer scientists from Stanford University, Sandy Lerner and Leonard Bosack, the company is responsible for pioneering the concept of Local Area Network (LAN). Today, the multibillion-dollar company has continued to set the pace in networking.

CISCO networking technologies

To its credit, Cisco has developed and promoted a long list of networking technologies. Some of the networking technologies promoted and taught by the foremost networking company includes:

Entry (CCENT)

The Cisco Certified Entry Networking Technicians is the lowest certification level offered by this company. This certification covers the fundamental networking knowledge, and CCENT certified individuals can perform some operations such as installation, management, and troubleshooting on small enterprise networks. They can also carry out some basic network security on such networks as well. Having a CCENT certification is the prerequisite for CCNA certification in order to enable a potential networker to understand the rudiments of networking before dabbling into it. In 2017, the company introduced two new examinations, ICND1 and ICND2, that prepare potential networkers in advanced for CCNA. It also prepares such individuals for CCNA Voice, CCNA Security, and CCNA Wireless.

Another entry-level certification is the Cisco Certified Technicians (CCT). This certification empowers technicians certified by the company to diagnose Cisco networking challenges. They can also restore and repair the network after a successful diagnosis. The technicians work in alliance with the Cisco Technical Assistance Center (CTAC) for prompt resolution of support incidents. There are two domains for individuals who are interested in CCT certification. These are:

- CCT Routing and Switching, a program that is valid for 3 years
- CCT Data Center, also valid for 3 years as well

The 3-year validity period requires that certification holders must register for same level Cisco recertification exams or recertification exams at a higher level and pass the exams every 3 years to retain their certification.

Cisco home networking

As a part of its effort to make networking easier and easily applicable to all facets of our lives, Cisco went ahead to incorporate home networking into the industry. This affords a homeowner to fully enjoy the benefits of networking.

Cisco Packet Tracer

The Cisco Packet Tracer is a very powerful and innovative networking simulation tool. This efficient tool is used for practicing networking and troubleshooting networking problems. Cisco systems designed this tool for creating network topologies as well as imitating the existing computer networks. With this system, you can easily simulate how Cisco switches and routers are created through a command line interface that is equally simulated. Through its drag and drop feature, users can easily remove or add network devices according to their specific needs.

Thus, the tool can be used for stimulating home networking and get mastery over the concept before putting your networking skills to use. The tool will assist you to understand some concepts such as IT essentials, Cybersecurity essentials, Networking essentials, and other networking concepts you learn during your networking classes. This will have a positive impact on your networking skills in the long run as you convert your home into a mini-networking project.

CHAPTER 13. • The OSI model

To make ideal use of applications that need almost real-time service, a network administrator should use the 802.11 standards. This standard includes a coordination functionality that provides a different way of accessing the wireless network. PCF is defined as the point of coordination function. PCF makes it possible for an 802.11 network to provide forced access to the medium. In some cases, accessing the medium under the PCF is like accessing the medium using a token.

The PCF is not widely used because, in the past, a media server implemented PCF although it was not successful. Certain enterprise-class products use PCF because it provides the access point's additional control over access to wireless connections. Additionally, PCF helps the wireless network to wrest control away from individual network stations. If contention-free delivery is necessary, PCF can be implemented for optimal results. Note that PCF is optional for the 802.11 standards. It is not mandatory for products to use PCF. However, PCF was designed by the IEEE specifically for stations that use the distributed coordination function.

Detailed PCF Framing

The contention-free period uses several kinds of frames that are exclusive. They come together in varying states known as:

- Polling
- Acknowledgment
- Data transmission

This chapter explains how different types of frames are incorporated and the way various functions combine during transmissions of frames. Contention-free frames usually combine several functionalities into one frame.

Data+CF-ACK

It is a frame that combines two functions for efficiency during the transmission. Information is channeled in the payload of the frame, and the frame confirms the receipt of information. Normally, the information and confirmation are required for two separate network stations. The free contention confirmation is focused on the information for relaying to a previous frame's access point.

CF-ACK

If only confirmation is needed, a frame with a header only on the CF-ACK function can be relayed. CF-Poll can transmit information by itself. Normally, it is only access points that can relay information from one wireless network to another. "Naked" CF-Polls are transferred when the access points have no buffered information for the recipients and do not need to confirm receipt of the other frames. A common circumstance when no confirmation is required each moment the access points exchange a CF-Poll. Also, sometimes the polled network station does not have information and doesn't respond. Whenever the access points do not have information for the next network station, they transmit a CF-Poll.

Power management and the PCF

CSMA is the fundamental technique used by wireless connections to share access to a medium. IEEE 802.11's standard protocol is designed to overcome the loss of power as a result of fame loss, which is caused by interference. Interference can emanate from any network stations that are not functioning correctly.

Using 802.11 on Windows 7

This standard has gone through enhancement through four versions. Every version is usually indicated by a letter at the end of 802.11 standards. From the newest to the oldest, they are 802.11 a, b, g, and 802.11 n.

i) Press and hold the Windows Key+Break for the system to open properties menu.

ii) Open the device manager by clicking on the link on the left named Device Manager.

iii) In the device manager, the pop-up box expands the region indicated Network Adapters. You will see two network adapters; one represents the wired Ethernet adapter (NIC) and the other the wireless adapter.

iv) Open the properties of the networking adapter item. If you have an 802.11n-adapter type, you will see several entries for 802.11n settings. They acknowledge that the adapter is 802.11n-acceptable, which implies that it can communicate with older 802.11g as well as with 802.11b wireless networking computers.

Pros and cons of different wireless standards are shown in the diagram below:

Wireless Standards 802.11ac, 802.11n, and 802.11g		
	✓ PROS	CONS
802.11ac	Fastest maximum speed and best signal range; on par with standard wired connections	Most expensive to implement; performance improvements only noticeable in high-bandwidth applications
802.11n	Significant bandwidth improvement from previous standards; wide support across devices and network gear	More expensive to implement than 802.11g; use of multiple signals may interfere with nearby 802.11b/g based networks
802.11g	Supported by essentially all wireless devices and network equipment in use today; least expensive option	Entire network slows to match any 802.11b devices on the network; slowest/oldest standard still in use

Using 802.11 on Windows 10

802.11 is an IEEE network standard that regulates wireless network relaying techniques. They are available in the versions below to provide wireless connectivity in environments such as homes and businesses.

1. 802.11n
2. 802.11g

3. 802.11b

4. 802.11a

802.11n which is the latest version is a non-wired standard that has many antennas to improve the rate of data transfer. The throughput of this version is affected by rate, interference from other networks, and the network setup. If you notice that your WIFI network is not working for any reason, use the following procedure to look at the settings for 802.11n connections and re-enable it if required.

Enable 802.11n for Windows 10

Click the Wireless-fidelity icon available on your Windows 10 taskbar and choose 'Open Network and Sharing Center' option. Click on change adapter settings. Select the properties for the WIFI adapter and then under advanced tab search for 802.11. Select it and change its value to "Enabled."

Windows computer authentication

When you authenticate something, the objective is to confirm that it is genuine. In computer networking, authentication refers to the process of proving identity to an application on the connection or network or a resource. Generally, identity is verified by a cryptographic operation that uses a key that is only known to the user. The server side of the authentication makes a comparison of the shared information with a known cryptographic key to verify the authentication attempt.

Cryptographic keys are usually stored in a central location to make the authentication process maintainable and scalable. An active directory is the standard recognized technology for storing identity data that includes the cryptographic keys. Kerberos and NTLM implementations require an active directory. Windows authentication methods range from a simple login to the operating system or a sign in to an application or a service. This method identifies users based on something that only the user knows such as a password or tokens.

Using 802.11 on Macintosh

Many computer users connect their MAC computers to a wireless network and do not bother much about the type of 802.11 protocol that is in use. Network administrators and advanced users are keen to find out the version of

802.11 in use to optimize speed and range coverage. Every wireless standard varies with different ranges. Besides, they provide different WLAN connection speeds.

The easiest way to find out the 802.11 standards being used by your computer is to check the advanced wireless fidelity information within the wireless section in Mac OS. You may check the wireless standard currently in use by doing the following:

- Press the OPTIONS button and hold it down and click on the wireless icon in the menu bar
- Determine the wireless router that is currently connected and search for the PHY mode in the menu

In the diagram shown below, the current router uses the 802.11n wireless protocol as shown. PHY is an abbreviation for the physical layer, which refers to the OSI communication model lowest level.

CHAPTER 14. • Wireless Network Applications

Since its introduction into the networking industry, wireless networks have taken the industry by storm. From the real estate to insurance industry, education to finance, wireless networking has continued to be the go-to technology when considering networking and Internet connectivity. Over the years, wireless networking has come in different forms and applications. Let's consider a couple of these types and applications.

Types of wireless networks and their applications

Wireless technology has gradually become an integral part of our daily existence. Most students today have a Personal Digital Assistant (PDA) or a cell phone they use for checking emails, voice communications, and other important uses. Thus, this technology has provided users with incredible opportunities that are too numerous to ignore as well as various beneficial applications.

Some public applications of wireless networks include:

- **Internet access:** An unlimited access to the Internet ranks high among the numerous areas of applications of wireless networks. It is easily the most compelling reason why installing a wireless network becomes a necessity. As earlier highlighted, having free access to the Internet makes job execution faster, is more convenient, and saves money.

- **Voice over wireless:** The incorporation of wireless networks into the transmission of voice conversations is a welcome development and a beneficial solution for individuals who need to constantly be in touch with each other. When wireless networking serves as the center of combination of data and voice, it provides the users lower operating costs and mobility. This is obviously beneficial to the users. For instance, retail store employees may quickly locate clothes for a customer or check their inventory via a specially-designed wireless LAN phone. With the full support of the wireless LAN in the store, barcode transmission while taking inventory of goods is possible. Pricing with a handheld barcode scanner is also supported by the LAN, making this a cost-saving alternative for retail store owners. In a business setting, a business may similarly deploy their telephone system over a wireless network. Thus, employees can move around with their phones as a cell phone, making it easy for them to accept calls with a single phone within the facility.

- **Inventory control:** Wireless LAN has assisted companies to track and update their inventory without delay. Real-time tracking and updating have enabled accuracy and efficiency to increase in the business sector. For instance, it is possible for a wireless management solution to update an inventory as soon as the clerk stocks a product. The huge impact on the retail store with this new development cannot be overemphasized.

The same can be said of the manufacturing industry. Wireless networks make keeping finished product and raw materials statistics up-to-date easier than it previously was. With wireless-enabled barcode scanners, manufacturing employees' workloads are made simpler because the wireless network allows scanners to handle some functions such as checking or changing product prices. These scanners can also go through the stock to check the number of available products.

It is noteworthy that the adoption of wireless LAN for managing inventory leads to improved accuracy. The accuracy, on its part, creates tons of benefits. For instance, the clerks don't have to deal with voluminous paperwork since they enter their data via handheld scanners into their main computers. This reduced human error significantly, when inputting data and thus, the company can boast of accurate financial records. This is of great importance to manufacturing companies as accurate financial records ensure that they pay their taxes promptly and accurately, preventing the companies from being fined by tax offices for incorrect tax payment.

CHAPTER 15. • Wired Network Components

When you are setting up a wired network, it is extremely important that you buy the right components. This will eliminate the challenges of setting up the network, especially since the setup can be quite cumbersome if not done with the right components. The primary components of wired networks are discussed below:

Network adapters: Without a network adapter, connecting to a network is only a mirage. The adapter works hard to provide the interface between a device and a network. A network adapter is responsible for receiving and transmitting data on both a wireless and a wired network. Network adapters come in different forms.

- There is a wireless network adapter with an antenna attached to it. The objective is to maximize the adapter's potential to reach a wireless network. Some other adapters do not have the antenna conspicuously fitted to the adapter but have it hidden somewhere within the device.

- There is another type of network adapter that depends on a USB connection to connect to a device. Some of these adapters include the TP-Link AC450 Wireless Nano USB adapter and the Linksys Wireless-G USB Network Adapter. These adapters are ideal for situations where the device to be connected has an open USB port but not a working wireless network card. You simply have to plug the wireless USB network adapter (also known as Wi-Fi dongle) into the USB port and it will automatically provide wireless connection without manually opening your computer to install the network card.

- You also have the Ethernet Adapter for Chromecast. This Google product is a device that allows you to work on a wired network with Chromecast. This network adapter is the ideal option when dealing with a very weak Wi-Fi signal that can hardly reach the device. It is also used when a building doesn't have the right wireless capabilities.

- There are equally some network adapters that are not hardware but software packages. These adapter types are known for their ability to perfectly simulate a network card's functions. These adapters are usually called virtual adapters and have a huge use in Virtual Private Networking (VPN) systems. A network adapter that is used for wired networks usually comes with an RJ-45 port with either untwisted or twisted pair cables for networking. On the other hand, wireless adapters establish a connection with the work via an externally connected or a built-in antenna. Both of these network adapters work well with TCP/IP and some other popular LAN protocols.

Some of the credible adapter manufacturers are Linksys, TP-Link, D-Link, ANEWKODI, NETGEAR, and Rosewill.

Cable connectors: Cable connectors are very important in wired networks. The RJ45 is simply the most common cable connector used for that network type. The good news is that every computer with capabilities for networking comes equipped with the RJ45 port by default. Otherwise called "Ethernet port" or "network port," it is an essential component of wired networking. The RJ45 plug shares a similar look with a telephone plug, although slightly larger. It is used for connecting the Shielded Twisted Pair or the Unshielded Twisted Pair cable. The cable connector comes in different types listed below:

- **Coaxial cable:** These cables resemble TV installation cables. However, they are more expensive than the twisted-pair counterpart.

- **Twisted-pair cable:** The twisted pair wire is a high-speed pair of cables with high transmission capacity. This pair can transmit in excess of 1 Gbps.

- **Fiber-optic cable:** This is another high-speed cable on the list. It uses light beams for data transmission via glass-bound fibers. It is also a high-data transmission cable that can be compared with the other cable types on this list.

Network software: The network software is also an important network component that cannot be ignored. It is responsible for packaging data into segments before putting the packet into a packet. The packet contains both the destination and the source addresses of the packet in question. The receiving computer then takes over from there. It interprets the packets into some meaningful data before it eventually delivers the interpreted data to the right application.

Hub/Switch/Router: Either of these three is an important component of wired network as well. Without a form of splitter or the other, it is impossible to connect a computer with others. A hub plays this role by repeating incoming signals into a port out to its other ports. A cable is then used to connect each computer to each of the ports. Then, there is also the switch. This is an upgrade on the hub, its more sophisticated version. A switch only sends a signal to the computer with the arriving message containing the address of the computer. There is also the router. Routers are more sophisticated than the two above and can efficiently forward messages to different parts of the world. Most of the larger networks more often than not make extensive use of routers for handling their LAN traffic. Thus, these three perform almost a similar function but with different levels of operation.

Servers: Servers are some computers that hold programs, shared files, and the networking operating system. These servers are responsible for providing access to the resources that the users of the network need. Servers come in different forms: print servers, file servers, communication servers, fax servers, mail servers, web servers, and database servers, to name just a few.

Network Operating System: This is a program that runs on servers and computers, allowing these computers to communicate as members of a network.

Local Operating System: A local operating system also performs a crucial role in networking. It is the operating system that allows personal computers to print to a local printer, access files, and use the disk drives on computer. Some popular local operating systems are Linux, different Windows versions, UNIX, and MS-DOS.

Patch leads: These components are used for connecting computers and other devices and the endpoints in all the rooms you want to connect. They are also useful for connecting switches, cable routers, patch panels, ADSL routers, and Hub/Switch. Centralized servers and patch panels can also be connected together with these leads. When buying leads, it is important that you buy a little more than double the number of the component that you really need. For instance, if you need 15 patch leads, you should buy between 32 and 35 of these patches.

Back batches: These are plastic boxes that are sunk or mounted into the wall. Through the back of the boxes, you can connect the patch leads' cables and connect them with the Cate5e/6 module.

Face Plates: These are needed for making your room presentable. They are primarily used for covering the back boxes and thus make your room or wherever the back boxes are used presentable. You can easily snap the Cat5e/6 module into the plates to complete your job.

Punchdown Tool: Setting up a network is very easy because nearly everything you need has been color-coded. However, you can improve your efficiency by having the appropriate tool for the connection. For instance, there are 8 thin copper wires in the cat5e/6 module, and these wires must be connected to the models and patch panels in the room. The punch down tool will assist you in getting that done without much fuss.

Cable Tester: When you have 8 copper wires to connect during networking, there are chances that you may accidentally get the connection wrong, and that may cause the wires not to work properly. You can ensure that your cables are working in the correct order with the cable tester.

Modems: A modem serves as the interface between the available Internet connection and your computer, using a telephone line. The modem is not a built-in component but is a separate part that can be installed on the computer whenever it is needed. Although a modem is not necessarily designed for LAN, it is a requirement for some Internet connections such as DSL and dial-up. There are different types of modems. They are:

1. **Dial-up modems:** The dial-up modems are otherwise known as the Standard PC

modem. These modems have a data transmission speed of 56kb.

2. **Cellular modem:** This is the simple modem that is regularly used in a laptop for Internet connection while you are on the go.

3. **Cable modem:** The cable modem is an extremely fast modem type. It is 500 times faster than the dial-up or standard modem. The most popular cable modems are DSL modems.

Whether you are contemplating installing a network in your home or at your office, these are the basic computer network components you should have on hand. Some of these components can be discarded, depending on what you are out to achieve. If you want to lay your hands on a home network, the router is a good idea. It can also work as a switch.

CONCLUSION

This is a new wireless technology where light is used as the channel of data transmission in opposition to the use of wires and cables. However, it doesn't come without some challenges, too, primarily, security issues.

This book has covered all these subjects extensively and has highlighted both the benefits and challenges of wireless technologies. It has also given us an insight into what the world stands to gain from wireless technologies in the future.

These are salient points that keep reminding us of what the world holds for us. It is imperative that you and I take full advantage of these technologies and use them to the full. That is one of the ways we can enjoy life to the fullest; we have the technologies to get things done better, faster, and easier.

OTHERS Book By Kevin Morgan

Hacking Beginners Guide

The Basic Guide to Information Network Security and the Basic Concepts of Kali Linux

Computer Networking Security

Beginners Guide

The Guide to CyberSecurity to Learn through a Top-Down Approach all the Defensive Actions to be taken to Protect yourself from the Dangers of the Network

© Copyright 2019 by **Kevin Morgan**

Lightning Source UK Ltd.
Milton Keynes UK
UKHW020630291020
372446UK00012B/960